SIMPLY STORIES
OF JESUS

Dorothy Wigan

Onwards and Upwards Publishers

3 Radfords Turf,
Cranbrook,
Exeter,
EX5 7DX,
United Kingdom.
www.onwardsandupwards.org

This first edition published in the United Kingdom by Onwards and Upwards Publishers (2017).

ISBN: 978-1-911086-80-2
Typeface: Sabon LT, Castellar
Editor: Honor Clare Parkinson
Graphic design: LM Graphic Design

Printed in the United Kingdom.

Endorsements

I have worked with Dorothy over many years and been so blessed by her beautiful relationship with God and her compassion for other people. This book reflects both these qualities and I will treasure it for always.

Jennifer Rees Larcombe
Beauty from Ashes

As Dorothy helps us enter into these familiar Bible stories, the characters start to come alive and our hearts are stirred afresh as we come into a new understanding of their real thoughts and feelings.

Like Dorothy, let's allow ourselves to be transported there, and ask the Holy Spirit to give us new insights that will both inspire and challenge us.

Marilyn Baker
Singer / Songwriter

Simply Stories of Jesus

This book is dedicated to my
precious daughter Abigail and
my husband Colin.

Both have shown constantly,
over and over again,
their love for me.

Thank you.

The Spirit of the Sovereign LORD is on me,
because the LORD has anointed me
to proclaim good news to the poor.
He has sent me to bind up the brokenhearted,
to proclaim freedom for the captives
and release from darkness for the prisoners,
to proclaim the year of the LORD's favour
and the day of vengeance of our God,
to comfort all who mourn,
and provide for those who grieve in Zion –
to bestow on them a crown of beauty
instead of ashes,
the oil of joy instead of mourning,
and a garment of praise
instead of a spirit of despair.

Isaiah 61:1-3

Contents

Simply Stories of Jesus

Foreword by Sam Onyenuforo

I count it an honour and privilege to be writing this forward for Dorothy, as I have seen the progression from the short story Dorothy wrote for a women's gathering, into a story told on a CD with instrumental music in the background, and now into a book.

Dorothy has personalised these Bible stories, bringing the reader into the scenes in a very unusual way. I highly recommend this book and invite the reader to read, pause and imagine being part of the various scenarios being portrayed.

Enjoy.

Sam Onyenuforo
Pastor, Oasis Church, London

Introduction

When I started writing these short stories, I did not realize the impact it would have on my own walk with God. As I stepped into each of the biblical characters' lives, I experienced the pain, shame and grief that was transformed into release and joy after coming face to face with Jesus.

My prayer is that as you read these stories, you too will come face to face with Jesus and experience for yourself the unconditional love that Jesus pours upon you.

RELEASED FROM DARKNESS

A blind beggar receives his sight.

Luke 18:35-42

I am blind. Every day I am dependent upon others to take me to a place where I can beg for money to pay for food. Sometimes people are kind, and put generous amounts of money in my begging bowl, and sometimes, others come and steal the little that I have. Many times, children put things in my way to trip me up; I fall down in the dust, helpless like a baby while they run off, laughing at my despair. Then sadness covers me because of my complete blindness, and rage burns deep within me because of the taunts of people. They kick me out of the way, and speak to me as if I were nothing.

Today I am sitting at the roadside, just outside Jericho. This is usually a good place to sit, because traders and farmers come in to sell their goods and if they have had a good day, they throw extra coins in my bowl. I am used to hearing the noises of the people, the shouts of traders, donkeys braying, their hooves clattering on the cobbled stones, and the camels' slow tread as they pass me by. However, today there is far more noise than usual – the sound and vibrations of a great crowd approaching from the distance. I can feel it in the ground, and hear it like a rumble of thunder.

"What is happening?" I ask.

They reply, "Jesus of Nazareth is coming into town."

In desperation, I call out, "Jesus, Son of David, have mercy on me!"

There is so much chaos, noise and movement that I raise my voice louder. The people close to me tell me to stop shouting and be quiet. *Be quiet? I may never have a chance like this again.* I have heard that Jesus heals people with leprosy and that he heals everyone who ask him – even blind men like me.

"Jesus, son of David, have mercy on me!"

I scream as loud as I can, my desperation making me almost violent in my cries to him. In my heart, I determine that I will not miss this chance to be healed.

I sense the crowd slowing around me, and hear the murmuring of people wondering what is going to happen. I hear Jesus' voice calling me to come to him.

Those nearest me grab my arms and lift me up on my feet, no doubt glad to be the ones to bring me to him, glad to be able to get close to him. I know in my heart that he is indeed the Messiah, the promised one. As he speaks to me, my heart leaps.

"What do you want me to do for you?"

In naked simplicity, I cry, "Lord, I want to see!"

"Receive your sight," Jesus says, "your faith has healed you."

My eyes feel as though a skin has been peeled back from them. I open them and gaze into Jesus' face. He is smiling at me, his eyes alive with love and compassion for me. He knows that all the years of isolation, scorn and hopelessness are now behind me.

In a moment, my whole being is aflame with light, colour and gratitude. Hope, life and praise flow from me as I start to thank God, dancing and singing, so that the people around about me start to join in with my song of joy and worship.

Oh, the wonder of sight! All the joyful faces of the people around me; the vibrant colours of their clothes; the fresh blue of the sky above and the flying birds; and the shapes of the buildings. I stare amazed, drinking it all in greedily, then I turn back to face Jesus. His countenance radiates joy, power and love.

Surely, I will always remember the eyes of Jesus looking deeply into the very heart of my soul, setting me free from the darkness and misery that bound me for so many years, drawing me into the radiant light of sunshine!

FREED FROM CAPTIVITY

Jesus heals a crippled woman on the Sabbath.

Luke 13:10-17

Today has turned out to be the most amazing day of my life – although everything started out the same as any other day.

For the longest time, I was crippled so badly that eventually I was completely bent over; all I ever saw was the ground – the dust, dirt and filth, and the feet of people passing by. No one seemed to notice me; I was the hunchback that had been around this part of the village for the past eighteen years. My back had been slowly but surely bending towards my feet so that my whole world was ever shrinking. Colour, laughter and excitement had been lost to me. Sometimes when I heard a child burst into laughter, I longed to be able to look up and see the happiness, freedom and joy on their face, to observe the sparkle in their eyes and to see the small, even, white teeth in their laughter-filled mouth.

I could no longer see a field of golden wheat swaying in the breeze, nor the olive trees hanging with the weight of a good harvest of dark olives, the silver-grey branches ready to drop onto the dry brown earth. I remembered the wonderful sunsets, the sky ablaze with reds, mauves, oranges and blues, and the dying rays of the sun dipping down into the dark of night.

Today, as usual, when I made my way to the synagogue, there seemed to be a stir of excitement in the air. I asked what was happening and someone explained.

"It's the teacher Jesus; he is speaking to us all today. Many stories have gone around about this teacher, and it is said that he has healed many sick people. He has taught in the synagogue and confounded the scribes and Pharisees with his wisdom."

I went to my usual place and sat down, curious. Suddenly there was a hush as Jesus rose to speak. I was captivated by his voice as it was so gentle, yet he spoke in an authoritative manner. There was no sound except his voice. How I wished that I could see his face.

Suddenly, the gentle voice was calling me to come forward... Everything seemed to slow down and I was very aware of my fear. I started to tremble – was he really calling *me* up to the front of this huge crowd? Me, the one whom no one noticed, no one looked at?

People around me took hold of my arms and led me through the crowd, to Jesus.

The first things I saw were his sandaled feet and the hem of his cream-coloured robe. He spoke to me with power and grace. "Woman, you are set free from your infirmity!"

As he reached out to me and touched me with his hands, it was as if I had been struck by lightning; my body was full of fire, then I felt as if warm oil was cascading over me from head to foot. I felt the cold stiffness melting away and it was replaced by a wonderful warmth and wholeness as I stood up. *I stood up! I really stood up...* and as I straightened, my eyes rested upon his loving face, the first face I had looked fully upon for eighteen years.

How can I describe him? Tears fell; the joy in my heart was overwhelming; I was utterly renewed, a transformed woman. As I beheld his face, I saw his power, authority and love. I could see his compassion for me and his acute awareness of the extent of my pain and loss over so many years. I was filled with wonder, as the beauty and radiance of his love were focused entirely upon me. My heart and everything in me cried out praise to the living God. I was flooded again and again with waves of fresh joy as I shouted my praises to God and this man Jesus.

Later I heard the murmuring of the rulers of the synagogue. They were complaining that Jesus had healed me on the Sabbath.

Jesus then confronted them saying, "You hypocrites! Don't you untie your donkey from the stall and take it out to give it water on the Sabbath? Then how much more should this daughter of Abraham, who has been bound in her body for the past eighteen years by Satan, also be set free on the Sabbath?"

The rulers of the synagogue were covered with shame and embarrassment, but the people around me were all pressing towards me, hugging me and laughing at my joy, delighted at the change in my body and praising God for all the wonderful things that Jesus was doing.

I was alive, my heart lifted in worship and my body was renewed. I walked away from Jesus free, with my head held high, and filled with his love for me.

JOY IN HIS PRESENCE
(I)

Martha.

Luke 10:38-42

I look out and see a crowd of people walking towards my house. *Jesus is coming to visit us!* My heart is filled with expectation and joy, as well as a little apprehension; I want to prepare all the dishes that I know he likes. There will also be twelve of his friends visiting with him, meaning that I need to prepare enough lovely food to serve *sixteen people.*

I live with my brother and sister and we are all very glad to call Jesus our friend. He makes everything so special when he is with us. When I know that he is coming, I go to the garden to pick the freshest figs, pomegranates and oranges. Then I go to the market for the best vegetables. I plan the meals with great care and I am up before dawn to get everything just as I want for him.

Have we got the bowls cleaned? Are the flowers fresh? Have the floors been swept and dusted? Is everything laid on the table that we will need? Will Jesus notice that I have made a new loaf of bread with a special recipe?

"Come in, Jesus; come in, Jesus," I welcome him. "We are so pleased to see you. Come and sit down in the shade and I will get you a drink to quench your thirst from the dusty roads." As he walks in, a sense of joy fills the house. We are all so happy to have him visit us.

My sister Mary is so different from me. I know that she is just as pleased as I am that Jesus has come but all she does is get a bowl of water and kneel down to wash the dust off his feet. And in her gentle, soft voice she looks right into his face and whispers, "Welcome to our home." Her face lights up with joy that she is so close to her friend. Her eyes are shining; her whole face is filled with joy and laughter.

There is so much talk to catch up on but I cannot be listening to that; I've got food to prepare for sixteen people. I get the ovens hot to prepare the various dishes and, as I do, I feel increasingly resentful that my sister does not jump up to come and help me. She can see all I have to do, she can hear me clattering around with the dishes in the kitchen, and as I get more hot and bothered with all the preparations, I also become more cross.

It is always me that is in the kitchen; it is always me that misses the conversation because somebody must get the food ready. Don't get me wrong, I love it when we have people in for meals, however I wish my sister would not sit around daydreaming when there is so much to be done.

Right – that is it! I am going to Jesus. He will realise all that I have to do. He will get my sister up and into the kitchen!

I have had enough – and burst into the room to see my sister sitting at the feet of Jesus, oblivious to all else, drinking in every word he is saying. Jesus is looking down on her, smiling, and they both seem so relaxed and so at peace in each other's company. I glare at Mary. *She is so selfish, not being there for me.*

In a loud voice, so that everyone can hear, I say, "Jesus, why don't you tell my sister to get up and help me in the kitchen? Food does not prepare itself, you know. Tell her to come and do her share."

Jesus looks at me and with a voice filled with love answers, "Martha, Martha, you are getting so het up about things that are not really important. Mary has her priorities right; she is listening and loving me and I see that her heart is pure, and that is what I want in all my followers. So, my dear Martha, come and sit at my feet, let us just enjoy being together; forget the responsibilities in the kitchen, choose me, choose to sit with me and you will find that your satisfaction in my presence is better than any food or drink. Hunger and thirst for me instead, my dearest Martha."

As he speaks to me I realise just how much I want to be with Jesus. I want to listen to all his words of wisdom, his words of love to us, to me and my family. Yes, this is the place I want to be. All thoughts of the kitchen are banished from my mind. He looks into my eyes and I know he sees my true desire to love him, to listen and learn from him.

Jesus smiles and says to Mary, "Move over; make room for your sister here. Yes, *here,* close, at my feet."

JOY IN HIS PRESENCE (II)

Mary.

Luke 10:38-42

When we heard that Jesus was coming to visit us and stay for a meal, my sister Martha and my brother Lazarus immediately started to plan. They always want to make the day special for him, by preparing the best food, getting in plenty of wine and clearing the room so that there is space for him and all his friends to recline and rest.

When Jesus visits us, it is for me a time of deep personal love for him. All I want to do as soon as I am with him is to drink in all that he says and to laugh and to talk with him and his friends. I watch him notice everything, how he listens carefully to each person in turn, giving them his full attention. I see how each person blossoms in his presence. Just to be in a room with him seems to transform people.

I have always been the quiet one of the family; always been at the back of the room, watching others, happy to sit and be an onlooker, never wanting to draw attention to myself; but when Jesus comes I want to lavish all my love, respect and honour on him. What a joy it is to get Jesus to sit down and for me to wash the dust off his feet; to get the best perfumed oil to rub on his feet and to feel him relax in our company.

Now Jesus is here! I run into the kitchen and Lazarus has got the largest jug of wine, which he starts pouring into cups for our friends and guests. I grab the largest cup, brimming with wine and take it over to Jesus. He smiles at me as I give it to him and I feel everything in me melt with love for this man. He seems to read my heart and to know that everything we value as a family we give to him.

As all the people start to sit down, I find a place right at the feet of Jesus, as near as I can be. I gaze up at him and listen as he talks and laughs. I see the joy in his face, his beautiful eyes dancing and sparkling with an inner fire and joy.

Jesus looked down to me and whispers, "What have you been doing? Where have you been? Tell me all that has been happening in the family."

Surrounded by a happy buzz of joy and laughter all around us, I tell him about my days. He listens and nods his head in understanding as I tell him of some small family adventure. Sometimes he throws back his head and laughs, when I tell him about some incident that seemed a disaster in the kitchen, but all the while I am aware that he is totally at peace in the deepest part of his heart.

It is as though he is listening in his spirit to God his Father and communing with him, but is able to be in two worlds at the same time – the Kingdom of Heaven, where his Father lives, and mixing with us in the earthly realm.

Suddenly Martha storms out of the kitchen, all hot and flustered – she is glaring at me but directing her words at Jesus. In a loud voice which stops everyone else in the room talking, she cries, "Jesus, don't you care about me? My sister sits all day dreaming at your feet while she should be out in the kitchen helping me. She has left me to do all the work myself, and catering for sixteen people is no small task. Get her to move herself and come into the kitchen and make herself useful!"

I immediately start to get up but Jesus gently lays a hand on my shoulder to prevent me from moving and says, "Martha, dearest Martha, leave your chores, leave the heat of the kitchen, come and share with us; you need not be flustered and upset about all these things. Martha, I want you to sit with me. I will not let Mary be disquieted by this; she has chosen the best by being with me and it is my desire that all people will love me and want to take the time to sit, listen and learn directly from me."

As I listen to Jesus' gentle, loving words to my dear sister, all I can do is worship him and, as I do, new love rises in my heart for her. Then, while looking at Martha with a smile on his face and a sparkle in his eyes, Jesus says to me, "Move over; make room for your sister here. Yes, *here,* close, at my feet."

BEAUTY FOR ASHES

Jesus is anointed by a sinful woman.

Luke 7:36-50

Simon the Pharisee is giving a dinner and the main guest of the evening is to be Jesus, the new controversial prophet who, among other things, *heals people.* According to the gossip, whether it is the worst case of leprosy or someone who has been lame from birth, Jesus totally heals them. No wonder everyone is talking about him!

What I would give to be a guest there – to see him and hear what he has to say... But there is no chance that someone like me would be welcome.

Jesus is like no other man – and I have met *many* men. I am known as the local harlot, prostitute, slut; all these names are thrown at me by the men and women of the village where I grew up.

I know most of the men in our village; they have come to me – oh yes, even Simon – and when we are alone, how they flatter me, how they long for my body and my skills at lovemaking! But when they are out with their wives and children their eyes are averted; they don't even look at me. I see the contempt on the faces of the smug dowdy wives as they pass me on the street. Little do they know how many hours I have spent with these men, their husbands, who appear to be so respectable.

I am used to taunts and abuse by men. They all seem so self-righteous until they get me alone; then they fall down on bended knees and beg me to be nice to them. They cannot shower me with enough money or gifts and honeyed words so that I will satisfy them. When we are alone, they will give me anything – money, jewels, clothes – and I take everything they offer. I now have my own house and money which I have put by for when I got too old to attract men.

Men... How weak they can be! How easy to manipulate! *I hate them!* I despise what they have done to me. I would never trust any of them but I love the power this gives me over them, these men who so often despise me.

Jesus is different though. I cannot understand my feelings towards him. I feel drawn to him and I want to give myself to him – but not in a sexual way. I want him to have everything I value – I, who have taken everything I can get. I want to give my very heart to this man.

I am going to see if I can get near to Jesus at the dinner. I will take one of my most treasured possessions, a jar of perfume, which has taken me almost a year to buy.

The house is packed. Simon has obviously got nearly everyone of note in for the evening and I can see gate-crashers near the doorway and the windows, all waiting to hear and see what the prophet might do tonight. I have decided here and now to move in amongst the crowd and edge my way towards Jesus.

Soon I am standing close to him. I feel my heart breaking. This man is so pure, so clean, so good! When I think of my life beside his, I feel like a stinking leper covered with sores and weeping wounds. This man is a holy man.

Within my heart I start to weep; deep heart-rending wails of grief rise up from my earliest memories. All the pain, all the misery; all the feelings of degradation, filth and despair rack my body, mind and heart, and I fall down at the feet of Jesus, sobbing out my anguish.

I am now wetting the feet of Jesus with my tears, my nose is running and I am gulping mouthfuls of air. I feel a total and utter mess. Yet Jesus does not draw his feet away from me in disgust. He does not seem angry with me, nor embarrassed with what I am doing. There is no humiliation, no rejection from him; just love, total and unconditional love. He is not touching me, talking to me, or even looking at me but it is as if goodness, cleansing warmth and a cover of protection flow over me from him, like the warm rays of the sun.

Oh, I can just picture Simon's face – he is so cold, so precise and hates any public display of emotion. I bet he is thinking, "How dare this woman break into my house and ruin my evening! If this Jesus is who he says he is, he would not allow this slut of a woman to come near him, let alone touch his feet. Some prophet he has turned out to be!"

Oh Jesus, it is so wonderful to feel that you don't despise me. I feel you don't even condemn me. I am overwhelmed with love and gratitude!

Everybody else in the room is either furious with me or looking at me with total contempt. Well, let them!

I open my perfume jar and pour it over Jesus' feet and as I break open the seal, the scent of perfume fills the room. I wish I had so much more to give him. I want this man to have all of me. If I owned the whole of the village and gave it to him it would not be enough, so great is the love I have for him.

Then Jesus speaks – and as he speaks, it is as if he knows every thought in my heart, and not only mine but also Simon's thoughts. *God help me! Who is this man?* I feel he knows every one of us in the room, knows the deepest thoughts that we do not dare to speak out loud; he knows them; he knows the scorn that Simon is feeling.

Jesus now turns to Simon and says, "I want to tell you a story."

"Go ahead," Simon says. "We are all listening."

The story goes like this: "Two men owed a money lender. One owed five hundred pounds, the other fifty, but neither of them had the money to pay the debt. The money lender cancelled the debts of both the men. Which one would be the most grateful?"

Simon says, "That is easy; the one with the most debt."

"You are so right," Jesus agrees. Then he turns to me in front of everyone and says, "Simon, when I came to your house you did not show me the basic courtesy of washing my feet, but this woman has bathed my feet with her tears and dried my feet with her hair. You did not pour oil on my head as a welcome greeting but this woman has opened a valuable bottle of perfume and soaked my feet in it. You did not even welcome me with a kiss but she has not stopped kissing my feet. I tell you, Simon, this woman knows she has sinned and is deeply sorry, and every sin in her life has been forgiven, *every one*. The person who does not feel the need for forgiveness does not feel the need for repentance."

Now he is speaking to me. "Mary, your love for me has saved you. I have come to bind up your broken heart; to give you freedom from your past sins; to put upon your head, my precious one, a crown of beauty instead of ashes; to pour over you, my beloved one, the perfume of joy; and to clothe you with a garment of praise instead of mourning."

His words of hope lift my spirit and I am renewed in heart and mind. His love washes over me like liquid gold. I feel I am receiving and giving love at the same time.

Then he says, "Mary, your faith has saved you. Go in peace."

I stand up, conscious that everyone is watching. There is an awed silence in the room as I feel his eyes gaze upon me with love. I walk away from him a renewed woman; pure, clean, my heart healed, set free and filled with his joy.

THE LOOK

Peter's denial.

Luke 22:31-62

My name is Peter; I have been a disciple and close friend of Jesus for the past three years. We have shared so much together.

Recently Jesus warned us that he was going to leave us, and that we would all betray him and leave him to face death on his own.

I was dismayed when he said this, and told him that though everyone else may leave him, I would never desert him, no matter what happened. I would even lay my life down for him.

He replied, "Would you? This night before the cockerel crows to greet the dawn, three times you will deny ever knowing me."

I shook my head in disbelief and thought that this would be the one time that Jesus must have made a mistake. *I know myself;* I would not let my friend down.

Later, we all went to one of his favourite places, a garden called Gethsemane where Jesus used to go when he wanted some quiet time for himself to pray. We all held back as he went deeper into the garden to be alone.

When it had grown very dark, we saw a crowd of soldiers and priests come into the garden led by Judas. What was Judas doing leading the soldiers straight to Jesus? He kissed Jesus. We wondered what was going on – it looked as if he was betraying him to the soldiers; there was so much noise and confusion. They seemed to be holding clubs and wielding swords as if about to confront a dangerous and violent criminal.

Jesus was surrounded and led away to the high priest where the rest of the scribes and elders were waiting. I followed at a distance with my friend John who said he could get us into the courtyard where Jesus was going to be tried by the priests.

A fire was burning brightly. I can still smell the wood burning as the flames and sparks leapt up into the night sky. We stood huddled close together to get warm, our faces reflecting the glow from the fire.

Then a young girl who was a servant to the high priest came up to me, looked me full in the face and said, "You were with the Nazarene!"

I looked at her with scorn and exclaimed, "Me? I don't know the man! Be off with you!"

I moved away from the light of the fire into the shadowed alleyway where several people were hanging about waiting, wanting to know what was happening. We were talking together in the crowd and as we talked I was aware of a man staring intently at me, and I started to feel very anxious.

He shouted, "Hey! You were one of the men with Jesus. I am sure I have seen you with him."

"Man, you have made a big mistake," I retorted. "I am not one of his mob!"

I felt rotten, so ashamed – and *fearful*.

About an hour later another man came up to me and with an accusing finger pointed straight at me. He proclaimed with a loud voice that seemed to carry across the whole courtyard, "You certainly were with Jesus; I know I have seen you with him. Everybody, he is a Galilean. Just listen to his accent!"

The people turned towards me; I could feel their hostility and hatred which seemed to press in upon me.

Fear rose up in me. I felt the awful taste in my mouth as I started to get angry. I swore at the man and felt my face flush with rage as I shouted my denial of ever knowing Jesus. I glared at the crowd and stood in a threatening manner, ready to fight. The swearing fell out of my mouth like vomit and the crowd nervously edged away from me, leaving a gap that led into the place where Jesus was being questioned by the high priest.

At that very moment, Jesus turned away from the high priest and looked directly at me. When he did so, everyone and everything seemed to fall away, and it was just him and me. In his eyes, I saw all at once love, pain, grief, understanding and forgiveness; no condemnation, no accusation. That look was pure love, pure and unconditional love for me. I looked at him in despair and sorrow as I remembered my arrogant response to his words only a few hours before. Oh, could I tell him of the grief and the pain in my heart, that the man who loved me, believed in me so unconditionally, should be so terribly let down by me?

The hot tears fell down my cheeks, my grief overwhelmed me, as I thought of how I had denied ever knowing him. *How could I?* This was the man I had said I would never leave, never be ashamed of.

Oh, God! Despair; sorrow; bitter, bitter weeping racked my body as I stumbled out of the door and cast myself on the ground, giving in to my overwhelming grief and guilt.

Then, in the stillness of the dawn, *a cockerel crowed.*

THE TOUCH OF LOVE

Jesus heals a man with leprosy.

Luke 5:12-14

I had leprosy. Just to say the words caused me to shrink back in disgust, to lower my voice. I stank of open putrid sores. The disease was at an advanced stage.

When I walked through the villages to beg for food, people picked up stones and threw them at me to keep me away. I heard the high pitch of disgust and anger in their voices as they feared that they might catch this dreaded disease themselves. They loathed the horrible smell and fearsome sight of the sore scabs peeling off my body. I felt their anger, that I should dare to come near them and possibly infect one of them.

One day, I was walking through one of the villages when I heard a group of people coming towards me. One of the men in the group was laughing and talking loudly. He said, "Jesus, what is your message today?" *Jesus... Jesus...* I have heard that name spoken of in awe by so many people, and now here he is with his friends. I've heard that he has made blind people see, and those who could not walk run and dance in front of a large crowd. I even heard of a little girl who actually died and came back to life after being with this man, Jesus.

It was easy to see who Jesus was even though I had never met him before. He stood out from the crowd as he had a power and a presence about him that drew you to him. I felt hope rise in my heart, something that I thought had died in me many years ago. I fell down, my face upon the dusty road in front of the crowds. I felt such turmoil in my heart, hoping that this man could do something for me.

My heart was beating fast with fear, as I was so close to so many people. Would they kick me and shout obscenities at me for daring to come close to them and their friend, the man called Jesus?

I found myself pleading and begging as I had never begged before. "Lord, if you are willing, I know you can cure me!" Everything within me cried out, beseeching him to make me better.

Then I was amazed as he put his hand out and laid it upon my head with such love and tenderness. I was expecting blows from him, abuse from his friends and disgust from the crowds, however as he touched me, the power of his love flowed out of him into me.

"Yes, I am *so* willing to cure you," he said. "I want your skin to be clean from all the weeping and open sores."

As he spoke, I felt life surge through my body and warmth tingling in every part of me. I felt as if I had been reborn; my eyes could hardly believe what had happened to my body as I lay in front of Jesus. My skin became soft without a blemish anywhere; all the grey, dead tissue seemed to fall off and the stink of all the sores disappeared.

I lay there amazed, so filled with gratitude and joy, the warmth of Jesus' healing and love racing through every vein in my body. I rose from the dust, stood tall, and started to leap in the air. I was singing and tears were pouring down my face; joy consumed me. Such strength and new life were mine; I was now free from the curse of leprosy. I could have hugged and kissed Jesus. I was crying and laughing at the same time.

Then I was aware that all the people were laughing and slapping my back and hugging me. *Me?* The foul one, the unclean one, the one nobody dared even approach? Now they were hugging me, shaking my hands, even kissing me. How wonderful to be touched, to be hugged and accepted.

I turned to Jesus to thank him. The look he gave me told me that he knew me, he knew my thoughts and loved me; that somehow, he knew everything about me. I felt that to him I was so special, that he had come that way today just to see me and to heal me because he loved me. His face was alive with joy, light and laughter. I felt deeply blessed by the joy and freedom he had given me. He spoke to me, and his voice touched and healed all the pain inside of me, all the rejection and hatred that had been shown to me over the years.

The eyes of my heart were opened in that moment. I had not realized until then that I had been a leper inside as well as outside. My wounds had been poisonous and weeping, very deep, and raw – I had been so aware of everything – but as his hand had touched my body, his voice had touched my spirit and I was healed because he wanted me to be clean inside as well as outside.

Jesus told me to go to the priest to be officially declared clean. Could anyone ever know? Could anyone ever understand or believe what had happened to me on this day? I stood in front of him a new person, and walked away from him free.

My life has been transformed. I feel as I have never felt before. I am whole, renewed within and without. I want to tell everyone what Jesus has done for me.

REACHING OUT

The man with the withered hand.

Luke 6:6-10

It was the Sabbath day – one I will never forget. On that day, Jesus came into the synagogue to teach. We never knew when he was going to come, but when he did, everything was intensified: the hush of the crowd as they pressed in, not wanting to miss a word that he said; the indignation of the Pharisees and the teachers of the law as they huddled together to try and accuse him of some Sabbath law that he might have broken. The hope and hunger of the crowd, and the open scorn and disbelief from the teachers at everything Jesus said, made his visits quite an experience.

None of us had ever heard of a teacher like Jesus. He spoke of love and we knew he lived a life of love because of all the stories we had heard from people who had been healed. From miles around, without exception, they spoke of his compassion, his kindness and gentleness, as one by one, people who had been told they were incurable now stood up and spoke *and showed* what Jesus had done for them.

I was standing in the crowd of men on this Sabbath day. My right hand was crippled and had been for many years. I always tried to hide it because, to me, it was ugly, deformed, and useless. I hated the way people would stare at my hand, then look away as they caught my eye. It never once entered my head to ask Jesus to heal my hand. I would not dare to put myself forward with all the teachers of the law just waiting to pounce on him and tell him in loud voices that he had broken yet another of the Sabbath rules.

Jesus looked straight at me even though I was within a crowd. He seemed to know me; it was as if he looked into my heart. Then he instructed in a clear voice for all to hear, "Come here! Stand up in front of us all."

I was quaking with shock, embarrassment and fear, however I took courage, stepped out and walked up towards him.

In an authoritative voice, he said, "I ask you all, which is it lawful on the Sabbath to do – good or evil? To save life or destroy it?"

Not a sound was heard. Everyone's attention was fully focused on Jesus. He then turned from the crowd, looked at me and said, "Stretch out your hand to me."

I did! The power that surged through my arm and the heat on my hand were indescribable. I gasped, amazed, as I saw my hand – it was totally healed! I stared in disbelief and reached out to touch it. It was now beautiful, strong; a perfect hand.

I lifted my arm so that all the people in the synagogue could see that the hand that had been shrivelled and useless was now strong and whole. The place erupted as people pushed forward to see it. People I had known for years came and pressed my hand to their faces and we laughed together at my joy.

Soon I turned my gaze to Jesus and I saw the smile on his face at seeing my joy. I had not asked for healing, but he had seen me tucked away in the crowd and because of his compassion, he had healed me.

Joy filled me. I could not stop looking at my hand; why did he choose *me?* I was a nobody, just another person in the crowd, but *he saw me* and changed my life forever.

JOY FOR MOURNING

The widow of Nain.

Luke 7:11-16

Jesus was back! He was going round the villages teaching, telling us stories that made you think long after he had told them. He told us to love our enemies; how could we do that? He spoke of peace, he did amazing miracles, and suddenly blind people could see when he touched them.

Who would not join the crowds who flocked to hear him teach, and hopefully see him do the impossible things everyone was talking about? Would a hopeless blind man see today? Would Jesus heal a leper? The latest story I heard was that he had turned water into wine at a wedding. I should have loved to have drunk that wine, because the people said it was the best they had ever tasted. They had finished the story with a laugh, saying that he could come to their home any time he felt like changing their water into wine!

I was one of those who gathered to join Jesus and his friends as they made their way to Nain village. We walked and talked together, and lots of light-hearted banter flowed between the crowd.

As we approached the gates of Nain we saw another large crowd coming out towards us. It was only as we drew closer that I realised it was a funeral procession. I saw a coffin being held high on the shoulders of six weeping men. Walking alone, totally bereft, was a woman, stricken, her head thrown back, wailing and sobbing. I could see her deep anguish and despair; tears were falling down her face; her grief and sadness seemed to engulf her.

I turned to look at Jesus to see how he would react to this woman. He had taken in the whole scene. The suffering and grief etched upon his face told me that he was fully bearing the pain she was carrying.

Some of the mourners close to us told us that she was a widow and that this coffin held her only son. They went on to say that he had been everything to his mother; kind and helpful in every way. He had known how to ease the burdens of her daily life. Suddenly he had fallen ill with a fever that no one could cure and he had died. The people of the village just could not believe that the woman should have suffered so much loss: first her husband and now her beloved son.

All the people stood in respectful silence, watching Jesus. When he final spoke to the woman, his words went deep into our hearts. "Don't cry." His compassion and his awareness of her grief were complete in those two simple words.

He went over to the coffin and as he approached, the six men carefully placed it upon the ground. Jesus touched it, his voice ringing out with authority and calm. "Young man, I tell you to get up."

There was an audible gasp from the crowd as we saw the young man sit up. None of us could believe what we were seeing: *the boy was talking to Jesus.* Jesus held out his hand to him and gave him back to his mother. They embraced and kissed each other.

The mother just gazed at Jesus and clung to her boy. *How could this happen?* We all saw the coffin, we all saw the mourners, we especially witnessed the grief of the woman now standing with her son next to Jesus.

Many of the crowd were overcome with awe and fell to the ground in silent worship at what we had just seen. We were all amazed and kept shaking our heads, asking whoever stood next to us, "Did you *see* that? Did you see what I just saw?"

Joy was shared between the widow and Jesus; words were not spoken but I could see that she was overwhelmed by his presence and love for her. Her face became radiant as she burst out laughing and hugged her son, kissing him repeatedly.

From mourning to joy, the crowd shouted and sung praises to God. Dancing broke out and we watched as she turned back from outside the village gates towards her home, walking hand in hand with her son. Then the joy of the moment overwhelmed them both and they laughed and danced with complete abandon; we could not help ourselves but to clap, cheer and shout praises to the Messiah, who had raised the dead before our very eyes!

PRAISE FOR DESPAIR

Doubting Thomas.

John 20:1-29

I just couldn't believe all the events that had happened over the past two weeks. Jesus, the one we all thought and believed to be the coming Messiah, the Saviour of the Jews from the tyranny of the Roman government – he was dead!

Dead. It was more than a disaster; all our hopes and dreams were broken when we saw him abandoned by so many who had professed to love him. I saw him being jeered at by the crowd as he bore the heavy cross that weighed upon his shoulders to Calvary hill. I saw the sweat, I saw the agony he endured by the weight of the cross and the torment of the onlookers, as he dragged it through the streets. I saw the blood that trickled and blackened his brow as the soldiers had made the cruellest of thorn branches into a crude crown and rammed it onto his head.

As that dreadful day crawled slowly by, we followed Jesus to Calvary hill, hidden by the great crowd. There I heard the soldiers cracking coarse jokes to each other. The harsh brutality and utter lack of humanity, as they man-handled the three men to be crucified, horrified me. The crosses fell to the ground as each man finally collapsed under the weight.

Then the men in turn were thrown down, each onto their own cross. The soldiers spread out their arms and hands, and with a ringing blow the hammer fell onto the iron nail that was positioned in the centre of each man's hand. I will never forget the scream of agony as each nail was punched into hands and feet.

I saw the horror and disbelief on the women's faces; I saw the scribes' and Pharisees' smug looks of satisfaction that, at last, this agitator of the masses was now being put to death.

I saw the soldiers pull the crosses upright on ropes. I heard the dull *thump* as the crosses were dropped into the prepared holes. I saw the soldiers spit on their hands then spit on the ground as they moved away, the first part of their duty done.

The blood – oh, the blood of my friend Jesus – was dripping down from his hands and feet onto the barren earth, turning the base of the cross into a pool of blood. As the day progressed, the sky went black and I stayed rooted to the ground in horror and grief.

I had seen it, I remembered it all – and I believed that the horror of that day would be a scar upon my heart for the rest of my life.

I heard his final cry: "It is finished!" I saw his head fall forward as his spirit departed.

My anguish overwhelmed me. Jesus, Jesus, my friend, the one with whom I had shared my deepest dreams, the one I had seen do impossible miracles. Yes, I had seen them. Wherever I went, no matter how big the crowd was, I had been right at the front. I saw when the blind beggar received his sight. I was there when the woman who had a blood complaint was healed. I had seen her terrified face as she had pushed through the crowd and touched the hem of Jesus' robe – and the transformation from terror to joy. I could go on and on... The lepers who had so desperately cried out to Jesus to be healed – and they were! Not a mark or blemish anywhere to be seen.

"It is finished!" Jesus had cried, and all I could say was, "Yes, it is *all* finished." *What a tragedy!* No more Jesus. No more promised Messiah. No more hope for deliverance from our oppressors in Rome.

I could not stand any more grief. I crept away from my friends when they said that they would all meet later. The doors would be locked in the house, of course, because we were all terrified of reprisals from the Jewish high priests. I told them to count me out; I would not be coming.

Two days later, my friends clambered around me, all bursting to tell me that they had seen Jesus, that he had come through the locked doors and had spoken to them. *Spoken to them?* I guessed that they had not had enough sleep and were suffering from delusions from all the trauma. I knew Jesus was dead. I had seen it. If anything, I'd had the clearest view of what had happened. I had seen the final thrust of the spear go right through his side,

I had seen the blood and water gush out – and now they dared to tell me that he was alive!

Well, I for one would never believe unless I saw for myself. I wanted to touch him and kiss him; I wanted to see the wounds from the nails in his hands and feet, put my hand where the spear had gashed his side.

I thought that they had all seen a ghost. It stood to reason; men could not walk through walls and locked doors, but ghosts didn't have skin and bones. I thought they were all in trauma and shock, and I didn't want to talk about it as it was just too painful and too soon for me to cope with stories like this.

Eight days later, I was with all my friends locked safely in the house when suddenly Jesus was in the room. He literally stood right in the middle and said, "Peace to you."

My legs started to give way; I could feel the blood drain from my face. My eyes and ears could not believe that this was Jesus standing talking to us. My mind assured me that this was just not possible – yet here he was, smiling at us just as he had done before all this had happened.

Jesus then turned and looked right at me. There was no escape from his gaze; I was afraid that I would see anger, disappointment and rejection – but no! He still loved me. I could see it in his eyes; I could feel his love as if it was wrapped round me; I could hear it in his voice as he spoke to me.

"Thomas, come over to me! Touch me, kiss me, open my hands. Feel the holes where the nails have been. Go on, reach out, thrust your hand right into the wound where the spear struck my side."

I was totally broken and could only cry through scorching tears that rolled down my cheeks, "My Lord and my God!"

There Jesus was in front of me. He had heard every loud denial of my disbelief in the past two weeks; my grief, my despair, he knew everything I had thought. *How could I ever have doubted him?* In the past few days, I have been over and over the times I have seen things that were just not possible. Twice I saw Jesus raise up people from the dead; so why did I not believe he could be resurrected from the dead himself?

My heart wept at my hardness and lack of faith. I had seen Jesus forgive many times, as people fell upon their knees to repent, and now he had come to me just when I was full of arrogance, doubt and grief. It was *my* time to experience for myself the overwhelming love, grace and forgiveness that only he could give. He saw through me; he saw the glimmer of desire in my heart to trust him. Jesus spoke to me and as he did, assurance of his love for me and his abiding faith in me made me realize once again that he had come just for me. He had come face to face with me, for all my doubts to be banished and my trust to rest entirely on him.

This encounter was deep, so personal and just for me.

Jesus then said, "Thomas, because you have seen me and touched me, you believe. How great is the blessing coming to those who have not seen me but still believe!"

I thought of all the people I had heard begging Jesus to help them in their unbelief, and now with all my heart I cried, "Lord, I believe in you. Forgive my unbelief!"

Jesus smiled at me, drew me very close to himself and kissed me.

THE TOUCH OF POWER

The woman with the issue of blood.

Luke 8:43-48

There is a lot of noise out in the street and as I go outside to find out what is going on, I see hundreds of people all walking right past my house. There is laughter, talking and voices being raised as people see their friends in the crowd.

I notice the man who has drawn the crowds and instantly I know, even though I have never met him before, that it is Jesus, the man I have longed to see – *the miracle healer.*

There has been so much talk of a man who heals; there are stories of lepers being completely healed of the disease, not a mark or a scar left on their skin. I have even heard that he brought a man back to life who had been dead for three days. Can you imagine the fear, shock and joy of the people as they witnessed such a remarkable event?

I have been so desperate to lead a normal life but because of my constant bleeding, I was declared unclean by the priests. Could this healer help *me?* I have been to every doctor for miles around. Each one I have seen has had a different opinion as to the cause of my illness and has charged me for various treatments, all to no avail. Therefore, I am still in the same condition after all these years – but a lot poorer.

I heard that Jesus does not charge anything. *I have to see him,* to get close to him so that he can touch me and make me well.

My heart starts to pound with trepidation. Is this the day that I am going to be healed, at last? Dare I push my way through that great crowd to speak to him, to tell him what is wrong with me? *No!* I couldn't tell him what was wrong with me with all those people pressing in on him.

The crowd draws closer: old men, women and young men lifting up their children to be touched and blessed by the healer. Mothers with babies in their arms reach out towards this man; there are children pushing and crouching through people's legs just to be near him.

He is so different, his face so gentle, caring, and so full of love. He seems to be aware and interested in all that is going on around him. Happiness appears to flow from him – and it is contagious! I see men throw back their heads and roar with laughter and joy, and I feel that it is only because they are in the presence of this man.

I have to get close to him. I may never have a chance like this again.

The stories I have heard about him give me courage to dare to believe at last, today, that this man can and will heal me.

I start to push my way forward from the edge of the crowd. There are so many people and the men seem to tower over me, but when I ask to be let through, amazingly they move aside to let me get to Jesus.

My hands are sweating, my heart thumping, however I feel that all I have to do is reach out and touch his robe. I believe he has power. I already believed he can heal but now I believe he can heal *me too.*

I am nearly up to him. I can hear him talking to the people and his voice is so gentle and loving. It seems to renew my courage to press on through to him. I have never felt so afraid in my life, nor so desperate, as I cry out in my heart, *Jesus, please, please heal me!*

I stretch out my hand. I can just about touch the edge of his robe.

Then fire, power, love and strength surge throughout my body like a tidal wave. I know I have been healed; it is as if a seal has been placed over my body. I feel the flow of blood stop. *Dear God, thank you for this man, Jesus!*

Suddenly everyone has stopped. Jesus is repeating something and he has everyone's attention. "Who touched me?"

One of the men, who is obviously one of Jesus' regular followers, laughs and says, " *Who touched you, Lord!* All of us have; it's so crowded that we can't help but touch you!"

"No," Jesus replies. "This was a different touch."

He starts to look deeply into the faces of the people around him, then he turns and everything seems to stand still as he sees *me.* Suddenly it feels as though it is just him and me alone.

I cannot look into his face, I am so overcome with emotion: fear at being found out and joy that I know I have been healed. I find myself blurting everything out to him – but he listens carefully to me. Oh, the gentleness of this man as he touches me, as he lifts my face and looks fully into my eyes!

"Daughter," he is now saying, "because you believed in me and had faith to believe I could heal you, you *have* been healed. Go in the knowledge of my love for you."

I look up into his face and as I do, my heart leaps with love for this man who has made me well. My soul dances with joy as I look into his eyes and recognise his love for me. I have never felt so clean inside and out, and his power and strength seem to be bursting within me.

I feel full of new life, enveloped in love.

I walk away from him, totally free.

REDEEMED

Zacchaeus, the tax collector.

Luke 19:1-9

Today a new prophet came to Jericho. I had heard a lot about this man. He has amazed all the scribes and Pharisees with his wisdom; it seems many of the most learned teachers have tried to test him about his teachings. What would he know about the law? He is only a carpenter from Nazareth, but it is said he outwits them with his knowledge and leaves them all totally confounded.

He also heals people: blind men can now see, leprosy vanishes from peoples' skin and men who were violent and insane, bound by chains and running wild and naked, are now clothed and sit at his feet, listening to his teachings of love.

I really wanted to meet him, but I knew there would be so many people all hoping to see him. I thought that no one would help me to get close to the teacher; most people in this place know me and hate me.

My position in this town of Jericho is Chief Tax Collector. I have been involved in bribery, cheating and corruption and I have used every trick in the book to become a very rich man. All the tax money passes through me and so from every sum I have taken a portion. My name is Zacchaeus but I am called 'the dwarf', 'Stumpy' or 'Shorty' because of my lack of height. Of course, this is all said behind my back, but I feel the contempt of the people as I walk past them in the street. There is no respect for my position, and no respect for me because of my size and because they know I have been a liar and a cheat.

What did I care? Today nobody was going to push me out of the way, nobody was going to pretend they couldn't see me; I was determined to see Jesus.

The crowd was coming towards me and as I looked, I could see there was no chance of getting to the front of all the people. I glanced up the street and saw trees lining the sides of the road. This gave me an idea. I started to run ahead of the crowd and look for a tree I could climb. I could see one with lots of overhanging branches that would be ideal. If I swung myself up and clambered along the branch, I would be right over where the teacher would pass by...

What a crowd there was, filling the whole of the street, all trying to jostle their way closer to Jesus. I could see him coming from where I was now perched! He walked directly under me, then stopped and looked right up into my face. (I cannot sufficiently express the surprise I felt when he stopped.) Then he said my name; *he called me!*

"Zacchaeus, hurry down from that branch, I want to come to your home and spend some time with you. Hurry down!"

I nearly fell out of the tree in my haste to get to him! I laughed for joy, something I had not done for many years. That Jesus should want to come to my house, it was more than I ever could have dreamed of.

Nearby I heard people mutter. "Why is the teacher going to such a wicked crook of a man's house? He could have come home with me." "What's Stumpy doing having Jesus go to his home?" "It's always the same; the dwarf has probably bribed Jesus to go with him just because he is so rich. I bet Jesus doesn't know what a corrupt and evil man he is, or he would never step foot in his house."

As I stood in front of Jesus it was as if I was stripped naked. He saw right through me; he saw me right from the beginning of my life, all the lies, the cheating, the theft and deceit. As he looked, I knew I wanted to change, wanted to get rid of the stench of my evil way of life. I understood at once that because of him I *could* change.

It's so strange – when other people have looked at me, and I have seen their disgust and contempt, I have either bullied my way through or totally ignored them. I could not ignore *this* man. When *he* looked at me he saw me as I was and he somehow knew that now all I wanted was to be clean. There was no hiding from him, no bluffing my way because, amazingly, I knew that Jesus saw me as I was *and yet loved me!* He wanted to come home with me and spend time together with me!

I spoke up and said, "Lord, today I give half of my wealth to the poor. What I have taken by cheating and false accusation I will repay four times over." I was amazed that Jesus, the man whom everybody wanted to come to their homes, had chosen *me* to visit instead. Me, the dwarf, Stumpy. Nobody but he had wanted to cross the threshold of my home.

Jesus then spoke to me in front of the crowd, saying, "Today, salvation has come to your home because you are also a son of Abraham, for the Son of Man has come to seek and to save the lost."

Yes, today I am a changed man. It is as if I have been reborn; my desires are different, my attitudes have changed, and there is joy in my life. I have such love for this man, Jesus, who has set me entirely free from the past.

Welcome to my home, Jesus!

What Shall I Read Next?

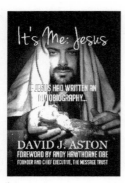

It's Me: Jesus
David J. Aston
ISBN 978-1-910197-25-7

The four gospels retold as Jesus might have told the story himself.

Join Jesus on a journey of friendship, laughter, revelation and hardships. Follow him on the donkey into Jerusalem. Listen as he talks about the creation. Watch as he restores people to health and wholeness. Accompany him on the hard road to the cross.

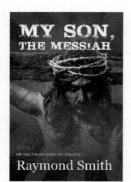

My Son, The Messiah
Raymond Smith
ISBN 978-1-910197-01-1

Throughout the whole Roman Empire it was what every mother dreaded: crouching at the foot of a wooden stake, waiting for your son to breathe his last and to bring to an end hours of excruciating pain and torture.

As well as the usual feelings that somehow it was wrong that the child should die before his mother, there was the confusion as to why my son, my firstborn, should be in that awful situation. Why was he being treated as a criminal? And not just any criminal, but on a par with insurrectionists? "How long?" was in everyone's thoughts, if not on their lips…

Books available from **www.onwardsandupwards.org**
and all good bookshops.